1965

MILESTONES, MEMORIES,
TRIVIA AND FACTS, NEW EVENTS,
PROMINENT PERSONALITIES &
SPORTS HIGHLIGHTS OF THE YEAR

TO :

FROM :

MESSAGE :

*selected and researched
by
mary a. pradt*

WARNER TREASURES™

PUBLISHED BY WARNER BOOKS

A TIME WARNER COMPANY

COPYRIGHT ©1995
by Mary A. Pradt
All Rights Reserved.

Warner Books, Inc.
1271 Avenue of the Americas
New York, New York 10020

Warner Treasures is a
trademark of Warner Books, Inc.

A Time Warner Company

DESIGN:
CAROL BOKUNIEWICZ DESIGN
PRINTED IN SINGAPORE
FIRST PRINTING : MAY 1995
10 9 8 7 6 5 4 3 2 1
ISBN: 0-446-91042-2

DR. MARTIN LUTHER KING, JR., LED FREEDOM MARCHES IN ALABAMA.

1965

IN OCTOBER, DAVID MILLER, A PACIFIST STUDENT AND MEMBER OF THE CATHOLIC WORKER MOVEMENT, WAS ARRESTED BY THE FBI IN VERMONT. THE FIRST TO BE ARRESTED UNDER A NEW FEDERAL LAW, HE WAS CHARGED WITH BURNING HIS DRAFT CARD.

Malcolm X,

the fiery intellectual Black leader who had broken with the Black Muslim organization led by Elijah Muhammad, was shot dead on February 21 in Harlem. He was about to deliver a speech about the need for Blacks and whites to live in unity and peace.

newsreel

In August, triggered by the arrest of a Black motorist and subsequent police brutality by Los Angeles police, race riots raged for 5 days in the Watts section of L.A. More than 30 people died, hundreds were injured, over 2,000 people were arrested, and millions of dollars of property damage destroyed whole neighborhoods. California governor Edmund Brown called in federal troops to quell the riots.

Rhodesia was on a collision course with destiny under Ian Smith, as he attempted to consolidate a white supremacist regime in a country with fewer than half a million whites and over 4 million Blacks.

headlines *international*

FERDINAND MARCOS BECAME PHILIPPINE PRESIDENT AT THE END OF DECEMBER. HIS WIFE, IMELDA, WAS DAZZLING IN CREAM-COLORED SILK WITH TRADEMARK BUTTERFLY SHOULDERS FOR THE SWEARING-IN FESTIVITIES.

Andy Warhol completed his famous "Campbell's Tomato Soup Can" painting; and "Op Art"—art that creates illusions using color, form, and perspective— becomes the rage.

cultural
milestones

THE FIRST SUCCESSFUL "SPACE WALK," 185 MILES ABOVE EARTH, HELPED NASA COLLECT INFORMATION FOR THE FUTURE TRIP TO THE MOON.

CONGRESS ISSUES AN ORDER STATING THAT ALL CIGARETTE PACKAGES MUST CARRY THE WARNING, "CAUTION: CIGARETTE SMOKING MAY BE HAZARDOUS TO YOUR HEALTH."

WESTINGHOUSE BROADCASTING'S WINS IS THE FIRST ALL-NEWS RADIO STATION.

"Amos 'n Andy,"

which began as a radio show in 1928, and became a successful television comedy starting in 1949, was pulled off the air after protests complaining about its negative stereotyping of Blacks.

television

"I SPY," STARRING ROBERT CULP AND BILL COSBY, WAS THE FIRST COP SHOW WITH A BLACK AND A WHITE PROTAGONIST ON TV. BILL COSBY WAS THE FIRST AFRICAN AMERICAN TO STAR IN A REGULARLY SCHEDULED DRAMATIC SERIES.

"Hullabaloo"

made a groovy debut in January on NBC. It was an outlet for rock-and-roll performers.

"A CHARLIE BROWN CHRISTMAS" AIRED FOR THE FIRST TIME ON CBS IN DECEMBER.

top-rated tv shows

1. "Bonanza" (NBC)
2. "Gomer Pyle, USMC" (CBS)
3. "The Lucy Show" (CBS)
4. "The Red Skelton Hour" (CBS)
5. "Batman" *Thurs.* (ABC)
6. "The Andy Griffith Show" (CBS)
7. "Bewitched" (ABC)
8. "The Beverly Hillbillies" (CBS)
9. "Hogan's Heroes" (CBS)
10. "Batman" *Weds.* (ABC)

most notable passage of 1965
milestones

Sir Winston Churchill

Perhaps the most notable was the death of this renowned British war hero and statesman, on January 30, 1965, at age 90. He provided the leadership and the symbolism (remember the cigar in his mouth and the two fingers raised in the victory salute) that got the Allies through the war. He recognized Soviet imperialism early on and popularized the phrase "iron curtain."

DEATHS

Lorraine Hansberry, black playwright, who wrote *A Raisin in the Sun* and whose play *The Sign in Sidney Brustein's Window* ran on Broadway in 1965, died of cancer at 34 on January 12.

Thomas Stearns Eliot, renowned poet, died at 76 in January.

Stan Laurel, the weepy half of the Laurel and Hardy team, died at 74 in Santa Monica, CA, in February.

Nat King Cole, singer, succumbed to lung cancer at 45.

Edward Murrow, patron saint of the Columbia Broadcasting System, died 4 days short of his 57th birthday, in April, of lung cancer.

Helena Rubenstein, multimillionairess cosmetics/beauty mogul, died April 1 in New York, at approximately 94 years of age. She had built a beauty empire with more than 100 products bearing her name.

show biz births

BROOKE SHIELDS, actress/model, was born on May 31.

SCOTTIE PIPPIN, basketball player, September 25.

DAVID ROBINSON, basketball player, was born on August 6.

KRS-ONE, seminal rap artist, was born in Brooklyn.

PAT CASH, tennis star, was born on May 27.

BRIAN BOSWORTH, football player/actor, March 9.

TYRONE "MUGGSY" BOGUES, basketball player, January 9.

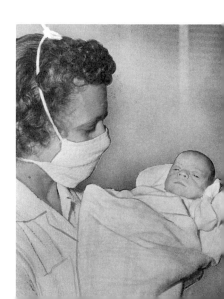

'65 hit music

TOP 10 SINGLES

1. **(i can't get no) satisfaction** Rolling Stones
2. **yesterday** Beatles
3. **turn, turn, turn** Byrds
4. **mrs. brown, you've got a lovely daughter** Herman's Hermits
5. **i got you babe** Sonny and Cher
6. **help!** Beatles
7. **i can't help myself** Four Tops
8. **you've lost that lovin' feelin'** Righteous Brothers
9. **downtown** Petula Clark
10. **this diamond ring** Gary Lewis and the Playboys

"This Is Where It's At!"
Columbia Records Beach Party
Miami Beach, Florida
July 16th, 1965

The Rolling Stones

had their first appearance on "The Ed Sullivan Show" in October 1964. In 1965, they took the States by storm.

bestselling fiction

1. **the source**
   james a. michener
2. **up the down staircase**
   bel kaufman
3. **herzog**
   saul bellow
4. **the looking glass war**
   john lecarré
5. **the green berets**
   robin moore
6. **those who love**
   irving stone
7. **the man with the golden gun**
   ian fleming
8. **hotel**
   arthur hailey
9. **the ambassador**
   morris west
10. **don't stop the carnival**
    herman wouk

In *The Psychedelic Reader*, Dr. Timothy Leary of Harvard advised readers to **"turn on, tune in, and drop out."**

nonfiction books

1. **how to be a jewish mother**
   dan greenburg
2. **a gift of prophecy**
   ruth montgomery
3. **games people play**
   eric berne, m.d.
4. **world aflame**
   billy graham
5. **happiness is a dry martini**
   johnny carson
6. **markings**
   dag hammarskjold
7. **a thousand days**
   arthur schlesinger, jr.
8. **my shadow ran fast**
   bill sands
9. **kennedy**
   theodore sorenson
10. **the making of the president, 1964**
    theodore h. white

Muhammad Ali, the former Cassius Clay, knocked out Sonny Liston about a minute into round one of a rematch in May. Few people saw the knockout punch, and so the World Boxing Association refused to acknowledge Ali's victory.

SUGAR RAY ROBINSON HUNG UP HIS BOXING GLOVES FOR GOOD.

PEGGY FLEMING, 16, WAS THE STAR OF THE U.S. FIGURE-SKATING CHAMPIONSHIPS AT LAKE PLACID.

CASEY STENGEL, 75, ANNOUNCED HIS RETIREMENT AFTER 55 YEARS IN BASEBALL. AT THE FAREWELL TRIBUTES, THERE WASN'T A DRY EYE IN THE STADIUM.

Sandy Koufax of the L.A. Dodgers pitched a perfect game against the Chicago Cubs on September 9, 1965. It was the 4th no-hit game of his career and only the 8th perfect game in baseball history.

sports

NO MORE RAIN DELAYS IN HOUSTON. IN APRIL, THE HOUSTON ASTRODOME, THE LARGEST INDOOR ARENA IN THE WORLD, OPENED WITH AN EXHIBITION GAME BETWEEN THE NEW YORK YANKEES AND THE HOUSTON ASTROS, WITH LBJ AN HONORED GUEST. THE ASTRODOME COST $20,500,000 TO BUILD.

TOP MONEYMAKING FILMS

1. *Mary Poppins,* $28,500,000
2. *The Sound of Music,* $20,000,000
3. *Goldfinger,* $19,700,000
4. *My Fair Lady,* $19,000,000
5. *What's New Pussycat,* $7,150,000

Julie Christie won Best Actress for her powerfully shallow role in *Darling.* **Lee Marvin** won Best Actor Oscar for *Cat Ballou.* Best Supporting Actor went to **Martin Balsam** in *A Thousand Clowns.* **Shelley Winters** was named Best Supporting Actress for *A Patch of Blue.* **Robert Wise** won directing honors for *Sound of Music.* Screenwriting awards went to **Robert Bolt** for *Doctor Zhivago* and **Frederic Raphael** for *Darling.* Best Song was the haunting **"The Shadow of Your Smile,"** from *The Sandpiper.* ***The Shop on Main Street,*** a Czech import, was named Best Foreign Language Film.

the sound of music WAS DIRECTED BY ROBERT WISE AND WON THE ACADEMY AWARD FOR THE BEST PICTURE.

TOP 10 BOX-OFFICE STARS

1. Sean Connery
2. John Wayne
3. Doris Day
4. Julie Andrews
5. Jack Lemmon
6. Elvis Presley
7. Cary Grant
8. James Stewart
9. Elizabeth Taylor
10. Richard Burton

movies

Imported-car sales increased significantly, with Germany's Volkswagen accounting for a majority of the increase. In July of 1965, imports reached the rate of 50,000 a month, with Volkswagen accounting for more than 35,000 a month.

cars of 1965

1965 was a record-breaking year for the American car industry, with manufacturers' passenger car production totaling 8,850,213.

Wolfgang used to give harpsichord recitals for a few close friends. Then he bought a Mustang. Things looked livelier for Wolfgang, surrounded by bucket seats, vinyl interior, padded dash, wall-to-wall carpeting (all standard Mustang)...and a big V-8 option that produces some of the most powerful notes this side of Beethoven. What happened? Sudden fame! Fortune! The adulation of millions! Being a Mustanger brought out the wolf in Wolfgang. What could it do for you?

Best year yet to go Ford

MUSTANG!
MUSTANG!
MUSTANG!

PRODUCTION OF THE COMPACT, SPORTY MUSTANG SOARED FROM 121,538 IN 1964 TO 559,460 IN 1965.

fashion

Geometric shapes took over. **Toplessness** continued as a trend. Whole lines of **"invisible underwear"** were produced, to give the illusion of nudity under sheer blouses or cut-to-here dresses. Because skirts were ultra-short, **the "leggy look"** was emphasized. **Lace leotards** and **textured stockings** were matched with sweaters, so the impression was of an all-in-one undergarment.

HOME-DELIVERED MILK

ACCOUNTED FOR ABOUT ONE QUARTER OF U.S. MILK SALES, DOWN FROM MORE THAN 50% BEFORE WORLD WAR II. THE FIGURE WOULD BE 15% BY 1975, MINUSCULE IN THE NINETIES.

final factoid

archive photos: inside front cover, pages 1, 11,13,14, 22, 25, inside back cover.

associated press: pages 2, 3, 5, 6,15,16,17.

photofest: pages 7, 8, 9,10,18,19.

original photography:
beth phillips: pages 13.

photo research:
alice albert

coordination:
rustyn birch

design:
carol bokuniewicz design
ginger krantz